SPOTLIGHT ON SPACE SCIENCE

JOURNEY TO THE MOON

LAURENCE DYSON

New York

Published in 2015 by The Rosen Publishing Group, Inc.
29 East 21st Street, New York, NY 10010

First Edition

Editor: Susan Meyer
Book Design: Kris Everson

Library of Congress Cataloging-in-Publication Data

Dyson, Laurence.
Journey to the Moon / by Laurence Dyson.
p. cm. — (Spotlight on space science)
Includes index.
ISBN 978-1-4994-0373-2 (pbk.)
ISBN 978-1-4994-0402-9 (6-pack)
ISBN 978-1-4994-0422-7 (library binding)
1. Moon — Juvenile literature. 2. Moon — Exploration — Juvenile literature. I. Title.
QB582.D97 2015
523.3—d23

Manufactured in the United States of America

CPSIA Compliance Information: Batch #CW15PK: For Further Information contact Rosen Publishing, New York, New York at 1-800-237-9932

CONTENTS

EARTH'S NEIGHBOR IN SPACE 4

THE MOON'S ORBIT AND ROTATION 6

WHAT CAUSES THE MOON'S PHASES? 8

WHERE THE MOON CAME FROM 10

MOLTEN CORE AND ROCKY CRUST 12

THE MOON'S LANDSCAPE 14

SHAPED BY ASTEROIDS AND METEOROIDS . . . 16

A SHADOWY PHENOMENON 18

A RARE SIGHT 20

OCEAN TIDES 22

SPACE RACE 24

THE LEGACY OF *APOLLO 11* 26

FURTHER EXPLORATION 28

GLOSSARY 30

FOR MORE INFORMATION 31

INDEX 32

EARTH'S NEIGHBOR IN SPACE

CHAPTER 1

Traveling through space at an average distance of about 238,855 miles (384,400 km) from Earth is the Moon. This rocky ball has been our planet's constant companion for about 4.5 billion years.

A moon is a naturally occurring **satellite** that **orbits** a **planet**. Earth's moon is simply called the Moon because until the Italian **astronomer** Galileo Galilei discovered four of Jupiter's many moons in 1610, people believed that Earth's moon was the only one in existence.

Today, we know of over 170 moons orbiting planets in the **solar system**. Some planets have many moons. Others, like Earth, have just one. These other moons may have been given more glamorous names, such as Titan, Ferdinand, Cressida, and Miranda. Our plain old Moon, however, has one very important claim to fame.

Its rocky, dusty surface is the only place in the **universe** other than Earth where a human has ever stood.

From Earth, the Moon looks as if it is shining with a white, yellow, or bluish-white light. The Moon has no light of its own, though. It looks bright because it reflects light from the Sun, just as a mirror reflects the bright light given off by a light bulb.

THE MOON'S ORBIT AND ROTATION

CHAPTER 2

As our planet Earth orbits the Sun, our little companion, the Moon, is orbiting Earth.

The Moon makes one complete orbit of Earth every 27.3 days. As it orbits, it follows an elliptical, or slightly oval, path. This means that sometimes the Moon is closer to Earth and sometimes it is farther away. These two points are called the perigee (when the Moon is closest to Earth) and the apogee (when it is farthest away).

Earth spins on its **axis** and makes one complete rotation every 24 hours. As Earth spins, the half of the planet facing the Sun experiences daytime, while the half facing away experiences night. The Moon acts

Moon at perigee

Moon at apogee

This diagram shows how Earth orbits the Sun (the white line), while the Moon orbits Earth (the red line). The diagram is not to scale.

in this way, too. The Moon, however, rotates much slower than Earth. It takes about 27.3 days to make one rotation. This means that a day on the Moon lasts for about two weeks. Then it is night for two weeks.

Because of the speed at which the Moon rotates, we always see the same side of the Moon from Earth.

CHAPTER 3

Sometimes the Moon appears in the sky as a thin crescent shape. At other times it looks like a giant white disk, which is known as a **full moon.** These changing views of the Moon in the night sky are known as phases.

We see the Moon go through different phases because as it orbits Earth, different parts of the Moon catch the Sun's light. You can see how this happens in the diagram to the right. It shows the Moon making one orbit of Earth. The inner ring of small Moons in the diagram shows how the Sun's light hits the Moon's surface. The outer ring of larger Moons shows what we see from here on Earth.

When we see a full moon, the Moon is on the opposite side of the Earth to the Sun. The whole surface of the Moon is lit up by the Sun's light, so the Moon appears as a shining white disk.

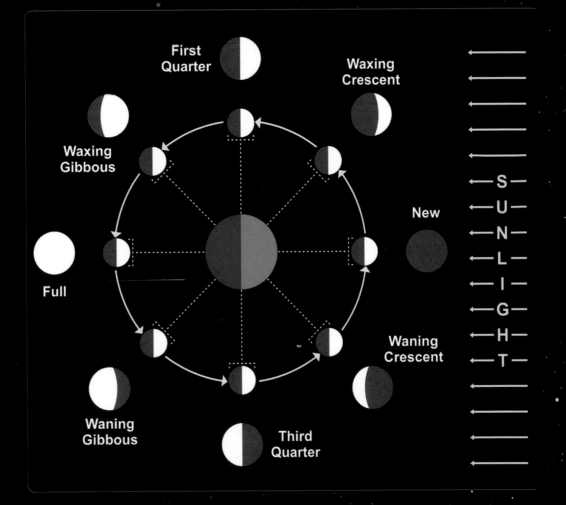

This diagram shows the Moon's phases during one orbit of Earth.

WHERE THE MOON CAME FROM

CHAPTER 4

Every object in the solar system, including Earth and the Moon, is orbiting the Sun.

The Sun formed about 4.5 billion years ago when gas and dust in a vast space cloud began to collapse on itself, forming a massive, rotating sphere, or ball. The material in the sphere was pressed together by **gravity**, causing pressure and enormous heat to build. Finally, the sphere ignited, and the Sun was born!

Leftover matter from the formation of the Sun clumped together to form the planets and other objects in the solar system. Then, when the Earth was less than 100 million years old, its Moon was born.

Over the years there have been many theories as to how the Moon formed. Today, most scientists believe a planet or some other space body the size of Mars crashed into the young Earth.

Superheated chunks of Earth and the impactor planet flew out into space. Over time this debris clumped together to form the Moon, which has continued to orbit Earth to this day.

impactor planet

Earth

This illustration shows how the Moon may have formed.

MOLTEN CORE AND ROCKY CRUST

CHAPTER 5

The Moon looks round, but it is actually shaped more like an egg. Scientists believe that, like Earth, the Moon is made up of different layers.

Deep within the Moon's center is an inner core of solid iron. This inner core is surrounded by an outer core of molten, liquid iron enclosed within a boundary layer of partially melted iron. Surrounding the core is a partially molten rocky layer called the mantle. The Moon's outer layer is a rocky crust with an average depth of 50 miles (80 km).

Beyond the Moon's surface, there is nothing! Unlike Earth, which is surrounded by a layer of gases, the Moon has no atmosphere. This means there is no air on the Moon.

The Moon's lack of atmosphere means there are no protective gases to shield its surface from the Sun's heat by day or to trap heat that can warm the surface at night. During the day, temperatures may reach 253°F (123°C). At night, temperatures can plummet to –387°F (–233°C).

thick atmosphere

no atmosphere

Earth

the Moon

While Earth has an atmosphere rich in nitrogen, oxygen, and other gases, the Moon cannot hold an atmosphere.

THE MOON'S LANDSCAPE

CHAPTER 6

When there's a bright, full Moon in the sky, it's fascinating to look up at our closest space neighbor and see the areas of light and dark on its surface. With telescopes and other imaging equipment, it's possible to see the landscape of the Moon in beautiful detail.

The dark areas on the Moon's surface are called *mare*, which is the Latin word for sea. They got their name because hundreds of years ago, the astronomer Galileo thought these dark

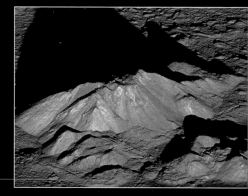

The lunar surface contains mountains, such as this 1.24-mile (2 km) peak in Tycho crater.

areas were seas. Today we know they are basins on the Moon's surface that are filled with a type of rock called basalt.

Basalt is **lava** that has cooled and hardened. Billions of years ago, parts of the Moon's mantle were superheated and molten. The liquid rock, or lava, rose to the surface and burst through cracks in the Moon's crust in just the same way that lava erupts from volcanoes on Earth. Today, there are no active volcanoes on the Moon. Now there are just vast, solid plains of basalt rock.

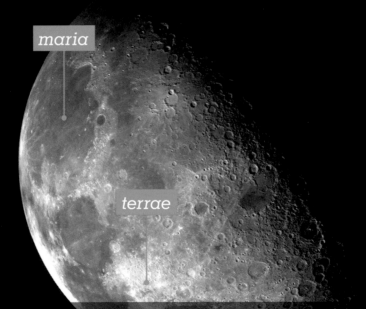

maria

terrae

You can see two major surface features of the Moon from Earth: the maria (the plural of mare) and the terrae, or highlands.

SHAPED BY ASTEROIDS AND METEOROIDS

CHAPTER 7

The Moon's lack of an atmosphere has helped shape its surface. Over the billions of years of the Moon's lifetime, hundreds of thousands of **asteroids**, **meteoroids**, and other space bodies have crashed into the Moon.

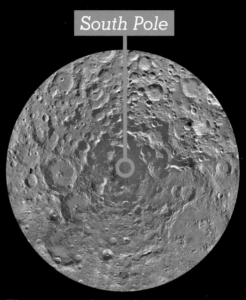

South Pole

This image shows the many craters at the Moon's South Pole.

These impacts happen because the Moon has no atmosphere to cause the space debris to burn up. The impacts have left the Moon's surface scarred by deep craters.

Scientists have estimated that there are around 300,000 craters of nearly 1 mile (1.6 km) in diameter, just on the Moon's near side. Many impact craters are hundreds of miles (km) in diameter and thousands of feet (m) deep!

All these impacts have also smashed and broken up the upper layer of the Moon's crust. The Moon's surface is covered by a deep layer of broken rock called regolith. The regolith varies in size from tiny dust-sized particles to huge boulders the size of trucks.

The Moon features craters of every size. Big craters are filled with many smaller craters.

A SHADOWY PHENOMENON
CHAPTER 8

An exciting phenomenon that everyone can see from Earth without the need for a telescope or special equipment is called a lunar eclipse.

As Earth moves around the Sun, it casts two shadows, called the penumbral shadow and the umbral shadow. Sometimes, when the Moon is in its full moon phase, it passes through these shadows (see Diagram 1).

The Moon doesn't pass through the shadows on every orbit. Most of the time, the Moon orbits above or below the shadows cast by Earth because its path is slightly tilted (see Diagram 2). Sometimes, however, the Moon's orbit takes it through Earth's shadow. This is when a lunar eclipse happens.

As a section of the Moon passes through Earth's umbral shadow, we see that area of the Moon become dark. This is called a partial lunar eclipse (see Diagram 3).

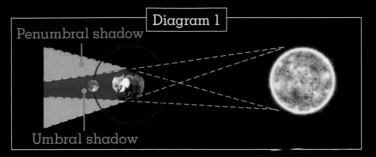

Diagram 1

Penumbral shadow

Umbral shadow

This diagram shows the Earth's shadows. The diagram is viewed from above and is not to scale.

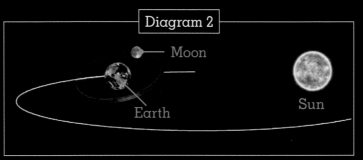

Diagram 2

Moon

Earth

Sun

This diagram shows how the Moon's orbit is slightly tilted to the Earth's orbit.

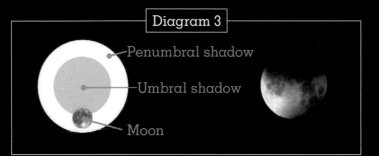

Diagram 3

Penumbral shadow

Umbral shadow

Moon

If we could see the umbral and penumbral shadows from Earth, they would look like two circles. Here, a section of the Moon passes through the umbral shadow (left). We see this as a partial eclipse (right).

A RARE SIGHT

It's possible to see a lunar eclipse from somewhere on Earth about two to four times a year.

Sometimes the orbit of the Moon is just right for the entire Moon to pass through Earth's umbral shadow. Then, a total lunar eclipse occurs. You might expect that the whole face of the Moon would turn dark during a total eclipse. In fact, the Moon becomes a reddish-orange color.

As the Sun's light passes around Earth, Earth's atmosphere bends the light. This enables some of the light to reach the Moon and illuminate it. The Sun's light is made up of many colors. Earth's atmosphere only lets through red or orange light, however, so that is why the Moon is lit up in reds and oranges. If Earth had no atmosphere, the Moon would appear completely black during a total lunar eclipse.

The "moment of totality," or moment when the Moon falls completely into Earth's shadow, causes the whole Moon to change color.

OCEAN TIDES

If you've ever spent a day at the beach, you have seen how the ocean's water level rises and falls. This change in water levels, called the tide, is actually caused by the Moon.

The Moon's gravity pulls things on Earth toward it. Solid things, such as mountains, only move the tiniest amount, so it's not noticeable. Water, however, moves easily.

On the side of the Earth closest to the Moon, the Moon's gravity pulls at the oceans, causing the water to bulge (see diagram, point A). A second bulge also happens on the opposite side of the Earth (point C) because the Moon is pulling the Earth away from the water on that side. On Earth, these two bulges of water are experienced as high tides. The water level rises by several feet (m), filling up harbors and coves and pushing the ocean further up the beach. As points A and C experience a high tide, points B and D have a low tide, during which the water level drops.

As the Earth rotates in relation to the Moon once every 24 hours, each place on Earth takes its turn to be in positions A, B, C, and D. So every place experiences two high tides and two low tides every 24 hours.

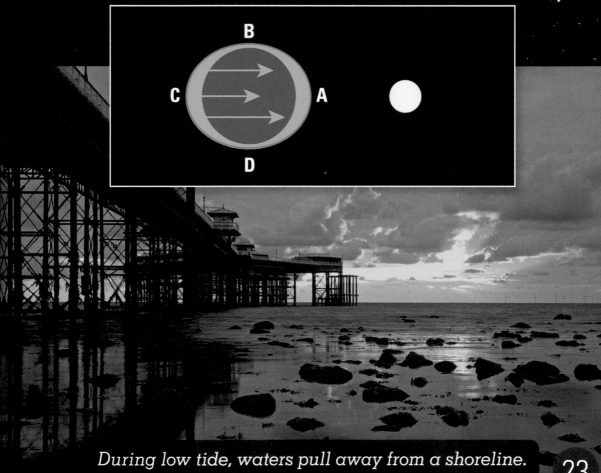

During low tide, waters pull away from a shoreline.

For centuries, the best way for people to study the Moon was by looking at it through telescopes. All that changed as a result of the space race. This was a competition that started in the 1950s between the United States and the former Soviet Union.

Some of the most exciting events that took place during the space race involved exploring the Moon. In 1959, the Soviet *Luna* mission landed the first unmanned spacecraft, called *Luna 2*, on the surface of the Moon. Later that year, *Luna 3* did a lunar flyby, sending back photographs of the far side of the Moon. The far side is always facing away from Earth.

The *Luna 3* spacecraft sent the image (left) of the far side of the Moon back to Earth in 1959. Fifty years later, NASA's *Lunar Reconnaissance Orbiter* captured the image (right) of the Moon's far side.

Viewing this half of our nearest **extraterrestrial** neighbor, a side that humans had never before seen, was an awe-inspiring event. But the biggest prize in the space race was yet to come. In 1969, the *Apollo 11* mission would send a crew of U.S. astronauts to the Moon, land them safely, and return them to Earth.

The Apollo 11 mission brought people to the surface of the Moon for the first time.

THE LEGACY OF *APOLLO 11*

CHAPTER 12

July 20, 1969, 4:18 p.m., Eastern Daylight Time. The event was the touchdown by *Eagle*, the U.S. *Apollo 11* **lunar module**, onto the surface of the Moon. This historical moment was the first landing of humans on another world.

Six hours later, with billions of their fellow Earthlings watching on TV, Neil Armstrong and then Buzz Aldrin became the first humans to set foot on the Moon. They stayed on the lunar surface for two hours

Footprint on the Moon.

and 36 minutes before returning to the *Eagle*. There, they prepared to blast off to rejoin the third *Apollo 11* astronaut, Michael Collins, who was orbiting above the Moon in the **command module**, *Columbia*. All three then rocketed back to Earth.

Eight years earlier, in May 1961, only weeks after the first human had been launched into space, U.S. president John F. Kennedy boldly set forth the following national goal: "before this decade is out, of landing a man on the Moon and returning him safely to the Earth." Tragically, Kennedy's life was ended by an assassin's bullet in 1963. In 1969, however, his promise was fulfilled by the *Apollo 11* Moon landing.

Buzz Aldrin stands next to the American flag the astronauts planted in the Moon's soil.

FURTHER EXPLORATION

Since 1972, several countries, including Japan and China, have sent unmanned spacecraft to study the Moon. In June 2009, NASA launched the *Lunar Reconnaissance Orbiter (LRO)* and the *Lunar Crater Observation and Sensing Satellite (LCROSS)*.

LCROSS was made up of a rocket called *Centaur* and a spacecraft that collected data. On October 9, 2009, *Centaur* was crashed into Cabeus, one of the Moon's craters. A cloud of debris from the impact rose nearly 10 miles (16 km) above the crater's rim. Instruments onboard *LCROSS* and *LRO* observed and analyzed the material coming from the crater. One of the discoveries was water in the form of ice crystals. This means that permanently shadowed areas of the Moon, such as deep craters, could be a significant source of water.

Centaur rocket

LCROSS spacecraft

Once LCROSS got close to the Moon, the front part of the spacecraft separated, rocketing into the lunar surface.

For decades, scientists have dreamed of building a base on the Moon that could be used as a staging post for missions to other parts of the solar system. The confirmation of water on the Moon, which is an essential resource for human explorers, brings that dream one step closer.

GLOSSARY

asteroid: A small, rocky body in space.

astronomer: A person who studies stars, planets, and other objects in outer space.

axis: The imaginary straight line that something, such as the Earth, turns around.

command module: The detachable control portion of a manned spacecraft.

extraterrestrial: Coming from or existing outside the planet Earth.

full moon: The Moon when it appears as a bright circle.

gravity: The natural force that causes planets and stars to move towards each other.

lava: Melted rock that comes out of an opening in the ground.

lunar module: A small craft used for traveling between the Moon's surface and an orbiting spacecraft.

meteoroid: A small body moving in the solar system that would become a meteor if it entered Earth's atmosphere.

orbit: To move in a circle around something. Also, the path of an object that moves in a circle around another object.

planet: A large, round object in space that travels around a star.

satellite: An object that moves around a much larger planet.

solar system: The Sun, planets, moons, and other space objects.

universe: Everything that exists.

FOR MORE INFORMATION

BOOKS

Hughes, Catherine D. *First Big Book of Space.* Washington, D.C.: National Geographic, 2012.

Lassieur, Allison. *The Race to the Moon: An Interactive History Adventure.* North Mankato, MN: Capstone Press, 2014.

Portman, Michael. *Where Did the Moon Come From?* New York, NY: Gareth Stevens Publishing, 2013.

WEBSITES

Due to the changing nature of Internet links, PowerKids Press has developed an online list of websites related to the subject of this book. This site is updated regularly. Please use this link to access the list: www.powerkidslinks.com/soss/moon

INDEX

A
Apollo 11, 25, 26, 27
atmosphere, 12, 13, 16, 20

B
basalt, 14, 15

C
Centaur, 28
Columbia, 26
craters, 16, 17, 28
crust, 12, 15, 17

E
Eagle, 26

F
full moon, 8, 14, 18

G
Galilei, Galileo, 4, 14
gravity, 10, 22

I
inner core, 12

L
layers, 12
Luna 2, 24
Luna 3, 24

Lunar Crater Observation and Sensing Satellite, 28, 29
lunar eclipse, 18, 19, 20
Lunar Reconnaissance Orbiter, 24, 28

M
mantle, 12, 15
mare, 14, 15

O
orbit, 4, 6, 8, 9, 10, 18, 19, 20, 26
outer core, 12

P
phases, 8, 9, 18

R
regolith, 17

S
solar system, 4, 10, 29
space race, 24, 25

T
tides, 22, 23